Teeth

By Debbie Croft

Illustrations by Wayne Bryant

Contents

Dr Fang

One morning I lay snug in bed,
The telephone it rang,
"This is a reminder
From your dentist, Dr Fang."

I fronted to the waiting room,
With fear and trepidation,
But even four-year-olds
Showed not the slightest hesitation.

The receptionist was smiling,
Her eyes full of disdain,
"That's quite all right for her," I thought,
"For she won't feel my pain!"

My knees, they knocked together,
And my palms, they dripped with sweat,
As I took the few short steps
That led into the dentist's net.

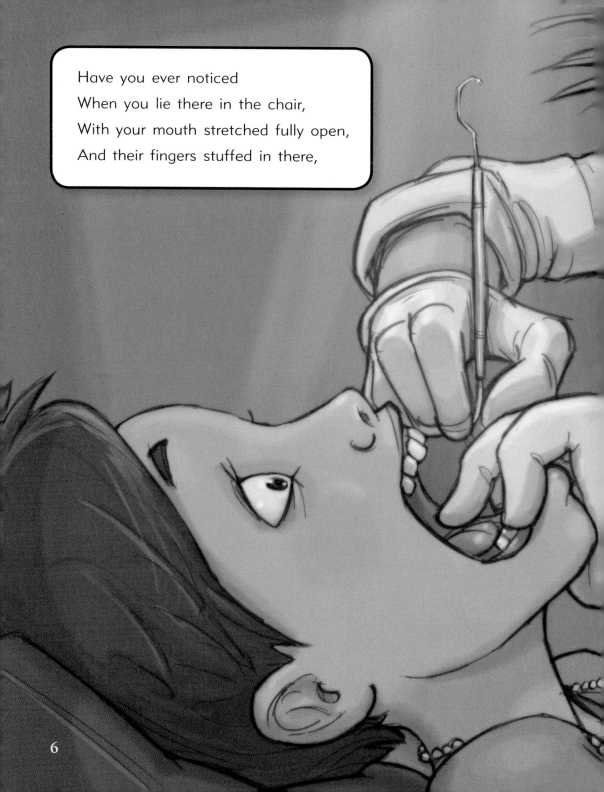

Have you ever noticed
When you lie there in the chair,
With your mouth stretched fully open,
And their fingers stuffed in there,

The questions dentists ask you
Rarely need a "Yes" or "No"?
They require a full-blown oratory
To make the answer flow.

But when my pearly whites
Had all the treatment they required,
He winked at me,
And ever so politely he enquired:

"Would you mind to scream out loudly,
So the patients can all hear?
Make them think it's painful,
So the waiting room will clear!"

He justified his comment with,
"I want an early mark,
My favourite team is playing
In the ball game at the park!"

Healthy Teeth and Gums

I believe one of the most important parts of personal hygiene is the care of your teeth and gums. A healthy mouth can affect your overall wellbeing. This is why you should develop good oral health habits from the time you get your first teeth.

The main reason you need to take care of your teeth and gums is because they have to last almost your whole life.

Today, many people are living well into their seventies or eighties. This means people will require their permanent teeth for a very long time!

If you do not care for your teeth when you are young, they could cause major health problems by the time you are an adult. Your teeth may even have to be removed and replaced with dentures. Both of these things make chewing and biting much more difficult.

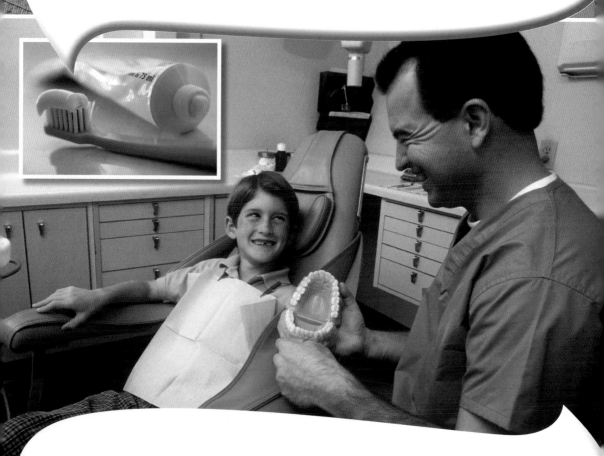

But with daily care and visits to a dentist every six months, most small problems can be prevented or fixed before they become major problems.

Also, poor health in your gums or mouth can contribute to poor health in your body. Infections that attack your gums can be carried through the bloodstream to other parts of the body. This can cause infections in places that would otherwise be healthy.

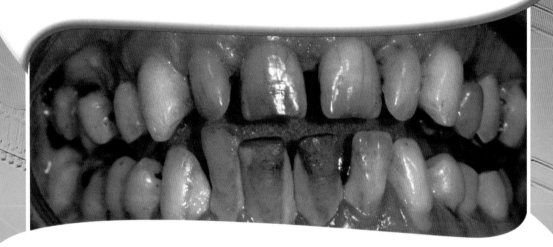

Strong teeth allow you to eat the correct foods for proper nutrition, and this helps you to keep your body healthy, too.

A healthy set of teeth can make people feel more confident. People with neat, well-cared-for teeth feel comfortable showing them off.

They are more inclined to laugh, smile and speak clearly when they are with their friends and family.

In conclusion, teeth need only a little attention on a regular basis. Remember to brush after meals, floss daily and have a check-up twice a year at the dentist. This can help keep your teeth and gums healthy, and allow you to enjoy good oral hygiene.